LINES ON THE UNDERGROUND

an anthology
for District Line travellers

Compiled by

DOROTHY MEADE & TATIANA WOLFF

Illustrated by Basil Cottle
and Jonathan Newdick

CASSELL

To Joe, Dora, Anna and Ben

*

And in memory of
M. M. W.

Cassell Publishers Limited
Wellington House, 125 Strand
London WC2R 0BB

in association with the London Transport Museum

This edition published 1996
The material in this anthology was first published in
Lines on the Underground, 1994

British Library Cataloguing in Publication Data
A catalogue record for this book is available from the British Library

ISBN 0-304-34841-4

Distributed in Australia by
Capricorn Link (Australia) Pty Ltd
2/13 Carrington Road, Castle Hill, NSW 2154

Printed and bound in Great Britain by Hillman Printers Ltd

DISTRICT LINE

Wimbledon

Great Wimbledon! You stand alone,
the queen of tennis on your throne,
with magic in your very name,
reaching world-wide with its fame,
history steeps your ivied walls,
echoing to the sound of balls . . .

And then at last the final roar
as one great player shuts the door
on his opponent, turns the latch
and wins triumphantly the match.
The crowd subsides, and peace descends
But not for long for soon it ends.
For soon again, with nerves strung taut,
Two other players walk on court.

H.W. 'BUNNY' AUSTIN* in *The BBC Book of Wimbledon Verse*
edited by Joanne Watson, 1987

*Wimbledon finalist twice and member of British Davis Cup Team, which won four times
in succession in the 1930s.

Wimbledon Park

. . . at last the great day dawned, with every Womble hard at work as
soon as the sun rose. . . . For the Midsummer party is the biggest, most
important and happiest occasion of the year.

At ten o'clock they all lined up outside the kitchen where Madame
Cholet, wearing a flowered apron, was doling out their party food. By
ten-thirty, with eyes shining and fur gleaming, they were lining up by
the main door, where Tomsk, looking very important, was on duty
with a list of names. At ten forty-five there was a rumbling noise and
Tobermory, wearing a flat cap, goggles and a long coat, appeared at the
wheel of the Silver Womble which bore the number plate: WOM 1.

He was shaking with excitement, but his face was dignified and grave as he picked up his first passengers, Great Uncle Bulgaria, Madame Cholet – now wearing a hat with flowers on it and a feather boa – Cousin Yellowstone, Bungo, Orinoco, Alderney and twenty-four of the youngest Wombles.

Slowly and very carefully the Silver Womble moved across Wimbledon Common beneath the golden light of the rising moon. Tobermory, who was always very thorough, had taken the time and trouble to study all the latest road maps, so he completed the journey to Battersea Park without a hitch, dropping his party at the gates at exactly midnight.

'Isn't it beautiful?' said Alderney.

'Not as good as Wimbledon though,' said Bungo.

ELISABETH BERESFORD, *The Wombles*, 1968

Southfields

George Eliot finished *The Mill on the Floss* whilst living at Holly Lodge, No. 31 Wimbledon Park Road [Southfields].

The London Encyclopaedia edited by Ben Weinreb
and Christopher Hibbert, 1983

East Putney

There was an Old Person of Putney,
Whose food was roast spiders and chutney,
    Which he took with his tea,
    Within sight of the sea,
That romantic Old Person of Putney.

EDWARD LEAR, *More Nonsense, Pictures,
Rhymes, Botany, etc.*, 1872

Putney Bridge

On the day appointed 'I came as one whose feet half linger'. It is but a few steps from the railway-station in Putney High Street to No. 2 The

Pines. I had expected a greater distance to the sanctuary – a walk in which to compose my mind and prepare myself for initiation. I laid my hand irresolutely against the gate of the bleak trim front-garden. . . . Swinburne's entry was for me a great moment. Here, suddenly visible in the flesh, was the legendary being and divine singer . . . a strange small figure in grey, having an air at once noble and roguish, proud and skittish. My name was roared to him. In shaking his hand, I bowed low, of course – a bow *de coeur*; and he, in the old aristocratic manner, bowed equally low, but with such swiftness that we narrowly escaped concussion . . . he had the eyes of a god, and the smile of an elf. In figure, at first glance, he seemed almost fat; but this was merely because of the way he carried himself, with his long neck strained so tightly back that he all receded from the waist upwards. . . .

. . . Watts-Dunton leaned forward and 'Well, Algernon,' he roared, 'how was it on the Heath to-day?' Swinburne, who had meekly inclined his ear to the question, now threw back his head, uttering a sound that was like the cooing of a dove, and forthwith, rapidly, ever so musically, he spoke to us of his walk; spoke not in the strain of a man who had been taking his daily exercise on Putney Heath, but rather in that of a Peri who had at long last been suffered to pass through Paradise.

MAX BEERBOHM, 'No. 2 The Pines' in *And Even Now*, 1920,
originally written for Edmund Gosse in 1914

Parsons Green

In a Village where I've been
They keep their Parson on a Green.
They tie him to a Juniper Tree
And bring him Currant Bread for tea.
A jollier man I've never seen
Than the one on Parson's Green.

ELEANOR FARJEON, *Nursery Rhymes of London Town*, 1916

Fulham Broadway

. . . In the Fulham Road near the Fire Station a shop had been con-verted into a tiny cinema. . . . It was called the Parsons Green Moving

Picture Theatre. . . . [It] seated an audience of thirty at the most, the front three rows of chairs being very small ones of the kind seen in nursery schools, and behind those (for the grown-ups) there were padded forms with no backs to them. Saturday performances started at 3 p.m. and the price of admission was twopence-halfpenny.

The music was provided by an old horn-type gramophone, operated by the ticket cashier, its horn protruding through a hole cut in the wall of the box-office. The films were all very short, and no doubt very old – they broke down many times in each performance. And at each breakdown a stout lady who always sat on a cushioned stool near the Exit . . . tugged at a little chain hanging from the gas-lamp near the door and, it seemed to our startled eyes, flooded the room with dazzling light.

C.H. ROLPH, *London Particulars*, 1980

West Brompton

It shone, pale amber, bluey-gray, and tenderly spacious and fine under clear autumnal skies, a London of hugely handsome buildings and vistas and distances, a London of gardens and labyrinthine tall museums, of old trees and remote palaces and artificial waters. I lodged near West Brompton at a house in a little square.

H.G. WELLS, *Tono-Bungay*, 1909

Earl's Court
Change for Piccadilly line, other parts of the District line and Kensington (Olympia) station

On 4 October 1911 Earl's Court received the first public escalators, or 'moving stairs', on the Underground. They linked the District platforms to the Piccadilly, but the public were wary of them and a man with a wooden leg, who was known as 'Bumper' Harris, was employed to ride up and down all day demonstrating how safe it was. Some old ladies were not encouraged in the slightest, because they had a suspicion about how Mr Harris had lost his other leg!

LAURENCE MENEAR, *London's Underground Stations*, 1983

High Street Kensington

A service at St. Mary Abbots, Kensington. The red plumes and ribbon in two stylish girls' hats in the foreground match the red robes of the persons round Christ on the Cross in the east window. The pale cruci-fied figure rises up from a parterre of London bonnets and artificial hair-coils, as viewed from the back where I am. The sky over Jerusalem seems to have some connection with the cornflowers in a fashionable hat that bobs about in front of the city of David. . . . When the congregation rises there is a rustling of silks like that of the Devils' wings in Paradise Lost. Every woman then, even if she had forgotten it before, has a single thought to the folds of her clothes. They pray in the litany as if under enchantment. Their real life is spinning on beneath this apparent one of calm, like the District Railway-trains underground just by – throbbing, rushing, hot, concerned with next week, last week.

THOMAS HARDY from his diary for 8 July 1888 quoted in
The Early Life of Thomas Hardy by Florence E. Hardy

There are more gates to the Gardens than one gate, but that is the one you go in at, and before you go in you speak to the lady with the bal-loons, who sits just outside. This is as near to being inside as she may venture, because, if she were to let go her hold of the railings for one moment, the balloons would lift her up, and she would be flown away. She sits very squat, for the balloons are always tugging at her, and the strain has given her quite a red face. . . . Returning up the Broad Walk we have on our right the Baby Walk, which is so full of perambulators that you could cross from side to side stepping on babies, but the nurses won't let you do it. . . .

. . . Well, Peter Pan got out by the window, which had no bars. Standing on the ledge he could see trees far away, which were doubt-less the Kensington Gardens, and the moment he saw them he entirely forgot that he was now a little boy in a nightgown, and away he flew, right over the houses to the Gardens.

J.M. BARRIE, *The Little White Bird*, 1902

Notting Hill Gate
Change for Central line

. . . the Gaumont Cinema at Notting Hill Gate has a ghost, which the staff nicknamed 'Flora'. The cinema was originally the Coronet Theatre and the ghost is said to be the spirit of a cashier who was caught fiddling the box-office receipts in the 1900s. When confronted with the evidence of her misdemeanour by the Manager she ran from his office, climbed the stairs to the 'Gods', and threw herself to her death from the balcony. A report in the *Kensington Post* in 1969 tells how staff meetings were so disturbed by the ghost when they were held in a room in the upper, disused, part of the building, that they had to be transferred to an office in a more frequented part. Footsteps came from the stairs leading to the sealed-off Gods, and occasionally a pair of small brown shoes were seen, climbing the stairs by themselves. The haunting usually occurs during Christmas week.

J.A. BROOKS, *Ghosts of London*, 1982

Yet here fashionable people buy little pastel-coloured terraced houses, and the bell-bottomed and caftaned crew of flat-dwellers talk about the place in affectionate diminutives. It is, simply, 'The Gate', as Ladbroke Grove is 'The Grove' – as if they were living in some model village in Wiltshire with retired brigadiers behind every elmed drive. Notting Hill Gate incorporates a central paradox of city life, in that its nature is as prolific and untameable as anywhere in London, yet for some at least of its inhabitants it has been accommodated to an order so benign as to be cosy.

JONATHAN RABAN, 'The Magical City', *The Times*, 26 January 1974

Bayswater

Just after you have crossed the [Serpentine] bridge (whose very banisters, old and ornamental, of yellowish-brown stone, I am particularly fond of), you enjoy on your left, through the gate of Kensington Gardens as you go towards Bayswater, an altogether enchanting vista – a footpath over the grass, which loses itself beneath the scattered oaks and elms exactly as if the place were a 'chase'. There could be nothing less like London in general than this particular morsel, and yet it takes London, of all cities, to give you such an impresssion of the country.

HENRY JAMES, *English Hours*, 1905

The troglodyte in a crowded tunnel under central London, watching District Line trains crackle past in procession to Ealing and Wimbledon, and waiting for the Circle Line train that never comes, can look at the map on the wall and daydream of far away places called Ickenham and Boston Manor.

PHILIP HOWARD, *The Times*

Paddington
Change for Bakerloo and Hammersmith & City lines

And yet, and yet . . . tomorrow I am going to London, and there is the old excitement, the prospect of so many pleasures, as the train noses its way under the Victorian roof of Paddington. Perhaps I have always been happy there, after all.

SUSAN HILL in *Living in London* edited by Alan Ross, 1974

This day, according to annual custom, bread and cheese were thrown from Paddington steeple to the populace, agreeable to the will of two women who were relieved there with bread and cheese when they were almost starved; and providence afterwards favouring them, they left an estate in that parish to continue the custom for ever on that day.

The London Magazine, 18 December 1737, quoted in *London in the News Through Three Centuries* by William Kent, 1954

Edgware Road
Change for Circle line

This was Haydon's* neighbourhood. His house was in Burwood Place a little street running from the Edgware Road (then still called Connaught Terrace at its southern end) to Norfolk Crescent. The house, which has also vanished now, was four-storied with iron railings round the area and pretty little balconies at each of the tall first-floor windows. It was on the south side of the street on the corner of the Edgware Road, overlooking a stream of traffic, which sometimes included Queen Victoria on her way from Buckingham Palace to Paddington Station. It was one of the noisiest situations in London, but when Haydon was painting he became so absorbed in his work that nothing penetrated to his consciousness of all the uproar of carts, carriages, barking dogs, street cries, banging door knockers.

* Benjamin Robert Haydon, the painter, in the month of his death in 1846.

ALETHEA HAYTER, *A Sultry Month: Scenes of London Literary Life in 1846*, 1965

Richmond

We [Estella and Pip] came to Richmond all too soon, and our destination there was a house by the Green; a staid old house, where hoops and powder and patches, embroidered coats, rolled stockings, ruffles, and swords, had had their court days many a time.

CHARLES DICKENS, *Great Expectations*, 1860–1

About noon he [Jolyon Forsyte] set out on foot across Richmond Park, and as he went along, he thought: 'Richmond Park! By Jove, it suits us Forsytes!' Not that Forsytes lived there – nobody lived there save royalty, rangers, and the deer – but in Richmond Park Nature was allowed to go so far and no further. . . .

JOHN GALSWORTHY, *In Chancery*, 1920

Kew Gardens

Come down to Kew in lilac-time, in lilac-time, in lilac-time;
 Come down to Kew in lilac-time (it isn't far from London!)
And you shall wander hand in hand with love in summer's wonderland;
 Come down to Kew in lilac-time (it isn't far from London!)

ALFRED NOYES, 'The Barrel-Organ', *Poems*, 1904

I am his Highness' Dog at *Kew*;
 Pray tell me Sir, whose Dog are you?

ALEXANDER POPE, Epigrams, 'Engraved on the Collar of a Dog which I gave
to his Royal Highness [Frederick, Prince of Wales]', 1737

There was a young curate of Kew,
Who kept a tom cat in a pew;
    He taught it to speak
    Alphabetical Greek,
But it never got farther than μû.

ANON., *Penguin Book of Limericks* edited by E.O. Parrott, 1983

Gunnersbury
Turn to page 13 for Turnham Green

Some cry up, Gunnersbury,
For Sion some declare;
And some say that with Chiswick-house
No villa can compare.
But ask the beaux of Middlesex,
If Strawb'ry-Hill, if Strawb'ry Hill
Don't bear away the bell? . . .

WILLIAM PULTENEY, Earl of Bath, 1674–1764

EALING BRANCH

Ealing Broadway

In May 1754, after a terrible trying winter, much broken in health, [Henry] Fielding 'moved to Fordhook, a "little house" belonging to him at Ealing, the air of which then enjoyed considerable reputation, being reckoned the best in Middlesex', writes Mr. Austin Dobson. . . . Full of exquisite pathos is the scene on the morning of Fielding's departure from Fordhook.

EDITH JACKSON, *Annals of Ealing*, 1898

On this day, the most melancholy sun I had ever beheld arose, and found me awake at my house at Fordhook. By the light of this sun, I was, in my own opinion, last to behold and take leave of some of those creatures on whom I doated with a mother-like fondness, guided by nature and passion, and uncured and unhardened by all the doctrine of that philosophical school where I had learnt to bear pains and to despise death. . . . At twelve precisely my coach was at the door, which was no sooner told me than I kiss'd my children round, and went into it with some little resolution. My wife, who behaved more like a heroine and philosopher, tho' at the same time the tenderest mother in the world, and my eldest daughter, followed me; some friends went with us, and others here took their leave; and I heard my behaviour applauded, with many murmurs and praises to which I well knew I had no title.*

*Fielding died in Lisbon on 8 October following.

HENRY FIELDING, describing his departure for Lisbon on 26 June 1754
in *The Journal of a Voyage to Lisbon*, 1755

Ealing Common
Change for Piccadilly line

Ealing Fair
Commences *Thursday June 24*, 1813.
The following PRIZES to be Play'd for, on the GREEN:
FIRST DAY.
A WATCH, Value £2 to be Play'd for at Single-stick
A SHIFT, to be Run for by Young Women.
SECOND DAY.
JUMPING IN SACKS, for **10.6d**
GRINNING through a **HORSE COLLAR**,
For a Large Leg of Mutton.
THIRD DAY.
Old Women Drinking Tea, for a Pound of Tea.
A PIG, to be Run for.
The first that catches the Pig and holds it to be entitled to the Prize.
A WATCH, Value £3, to be Play'd for at Single-stick.
A POUND of TOBACCO, to be Smoaked for.
To begin at FOUR o'Clock each Day.

From lantern slides in the collection of the Ealing Photographic Society,
illustrated in *Ealing* by Charles Jones, 1903

Acton Town
Change for Piccadilly line

By 1900 there were 180 laundries in South Acton, which was colloquially known as 'Soapsuds Island'.

The London Encyclopaedia edited by Ben Weinreb
and Christopher Hibbert, 1983

Chiswick Park

Sir Walter Scott, in his 'Diary', May 17th, 1828, tells us that . . . he drove to Chiswick, where he had never been before. 'A numerous and gay party,' he adds, 'were assembled to walk and enjoy the beauties of that Palladian dome. The place and highly ornamental gardens belonging to it resemble a picture of Watteau. There is some affectation in the picture, but in the *ensemble* the original looked very well. The Duke of Devonshire received every one with the best possible manners. The scene was dignified by the presence of an immense elephant, who, under the charge of a groom, wandered up and down, giving an air of Asiatic pageantry to the entertainment.'

W. THORNBURY AND E. WALFORD, *Old and New London*, 1873–8

Sir Stephen Fox's House at Chiswick, now possessed by the Earl of Wilmington, is a very fine and convenient Building; King William was so well pleased with it, that when he had seen the House and Garden, he said to the Earl of Portland, *This Place is perfectly fine, I could live here for five Days.*

DANIEL DEFOE, *A Tour thro' the Whole Island of Great Britain*, 1738

Turnham Green

All the angels at Turnham Green
Survey a gentle, idyllic scene –
Wide-winged, blue-eyed, English ones,
With their hair tied up in buns.
How lucidly they look – behold
Privet hedges green and gold
Round tiny gardens prettified
With stocks and pinks and London Pride,
Of houses built on a modest plan,
Semi-detached Victorian,
With freshly painted doors that shine
All along the District Line.
By Supermarket and Odeon
Celestial guardians march on. . . .

JOHN HEATH-STUBBS, *Satires and Epigrams*, 1968

Stamford Brook

From Wormwood Scrubs, Stamford Brook runs to Old Oak Common, touching the south-west corner of the Common, in the garden of the old Acton Wells Assembly Rooms, famous in the days of Queen Anne – when Wormwood Scrubs was infinitely more fashionable than it is today – for their purging waters.

The story of Acton Wells typifies what happened to so many of London's wells. They were fashionable until the days of the American Revolution. An advertisement on 3 July 1771 stated: By the recommendation of Physicians and the encouragement of the nobility and gentry Acton Wells are newly opened for the benefit of the public. Every Monday, Wednesday and Friday from Lady Day to Michaelmas are public days for drinking the waters and breakfasting.

RICHARD TRENCH AND ELLIS HILLMAN,
London Under London, 1984, revised 1993

Ravenscourt Park

O men of Kensington! . . . sword in hand, you drove the Empire of Hammersmith back mile by mile, swept it past its own Broadway, and broke it at last in a battle so long and bloody that the birds of prey have left their name upon it. Men have called it, with austere irony, the Ravenscourt.

G.K. CHESTERTON, *The Napoleon of Notting Hill,* 1904

Ravenscourt, though not large (32 acres), is very beautiful. With Waterlow, Clissold, and Brockwell Parks it shares the distinction of being a real park, centuries old; and despite the new features, the gravelled paths, garden-beds, iron railings, etc., which had to be introduced when it was opened to the public, it retains much of its original park-like character. Its venerable elms, hornbeams, beeches, cedars, and hawthorns are a very noble possession. To my mind this indeed is the most beautiful park in London.

W.H. HUDSON, *Birds in London,* 1898

Hammersmith
Change for Hammersmith & City and Piccadilly lines

One of the things I have always disliked about William Morris is that he is rude [at the start of *News from Nowhere*] about Hammersmith Bridge. For those unlucky enough not to know it, Hammersmith Bridge is a dignified Victorian structure, crowned with small but ornate pinnacles, which joins Middlesex to Surrey. When I was a child it was a source of intense and unmitigated delight. For one thing, being a suspension bridge it wobbled when buses went across. There you would be, clutching a parental hand high over the Thames, when suddenly the pavement would shiver and dance beneath your feet as a double-decker rumbled by. . . . Then there were the gulls. At Hammersmith, of course, the river is still tidal. On a good day you can smell the sea. At the ebb, wide mud-flats appear, and these would be covered, especially in stormy weather, with huge gulls. When you crossed the bridge, gulls would bank and glide under you and back and over your head. If you held a piece of bread over the rail, they would swoop and snatch it from your fingers . . . a safer idea was to take a bag of crusts and toss them in handfuls over the water. Instantly you would be the centre of a screaming, fighting white tornado. . . .

JOHN CAREY, *Original Copy*, 1987

Barons Court
Change for Piccadilly line

Earls Court
    With knee bent low,
Barons Court
    With a kiss and a blow.
I dropped a curtsey to the Earl,
    I'm the Baron's lady – O!

ELEANOR FARJEON, *Nursery Rhymes of London Town*, 1916

West Kensington

London moved me greatly because of the walks by the side of the Thames towards *Little Chelsea*. There were little houses there set off with rose trees that I found truly elegiac. It was the first time I was affected by the sentimental mode.

STENDHAL (M.H. Beyle), *Souvenirs d'Egotisme*, 1832

Earl's Court
Change for Kensington (Olympia)

And what has Earls Court got? . . .
A station (Metropolitan and Underground)
 Known to commuters as a terminal . . .
What Earls Court has is this:
A sense of free and easy. There are no Joneses
For anybody to keep up with here.
The negroes in the snow are beautiful,
And you can wear what clothes you damn well please.
No debs. No escorts. No tycoons. But life
In great variety.

GAVIN EWART, *Londoners*, 1964

Kensington (Olympia)

During the last spring and the most beautiful summer that has suc-
ceeded it, I have, with the exception of a mere gallop into Somerset-
shire and back, been constantly at Kensington*, occupied chiefly in
sowing and rearing American trees and shrubs, of which I have now, I
think, a *million* of various sorts, including about ten thousand apple-
trees. 28 July 1825.

WILLIAM COBBETT, *Rural Rides*, 1830

*Cobbett's farm was on the south side of the present High Street. In 1831, he said of it that
it contained 'two cows, a bull-calf, two old sows, five male pigs, and seven females, all
these about three months old, two cocks, ten hens, and about seventeen pigeons'.

Gloucester Road
Change for Piccadilly line

When they finally threw us out of Pommeroy's, and after we had con-
sidered the possibility of buying the Bishop brandy in the Cock Tavern,

and even beer in the Devereux, I let my instinct, like an aged horse, carry me on to the Underground and home to Gloucester Road, and there discovered the rissoles, like some traces of a vanished civilization, fossilized in the oven. She Who Must Be Obeyed was already in bed, feigning sleep. When I climbed in beside her she opened a hostile eye.

'You're drunk, Rumpole!' she said. 'What on earth have you been doing?'

'I've been having a legal discussion,' I told her, 'on the subject of the admissibility of certain evidence. Vital, from my client's point of view. And, just for a change, Hilda, I think I've won.'

'Well, you'd better try and get some sleep.' And she added with a sort of satisfaction, 'I'm sure you'll be feeling quite terrible in the morning.'

JOHN MORTIMER, 'Rumpole and the Spirit of Christmas',
Rumpole for the Defence, 1981

South Kensington
Change for Piccadilly line

It would not be true to say she was doing nothing:
She visited several bookshops, spent an hour
In the Victoria and Albert Museum (Indian section),
And walked carefully through the streets of Kensington
Carrying five mushrooms in a paper bag,
A tin of black pepper, a literary magazine,
And enough money to pay the rent for two weeks.
The sky was cloudy, leaves lay on the pavements.

Nor did she lack human contacts: she spoke
To three shop-assistants and a newsvendor,
And returned the 'Good-night' of a museum attendant.
Arriving home, she wrote a letter to someone
In Canada, as it might be, or in New Zealand,
Listening to the news as she cooked her meal,
And conversed for five minutes with the landlady.
The air was damp with the mist of late autumn.
A full day, and not unrewarding.
Night fell at the usual seasonal hour.
She drew the curtains, switched on the electric fire,

Washed her hair and read until it was dry,
Then went to bed; where, for the hours of darkness,
She lay pierced by thirty black spears
And felt her limbs numb, her eyes burning,
And dark rust carried along her blood.

FLEUR ADCOCK, 'Miss Hamilton in London', *Tigers*, 1967

Sloane Square

And you're giving a treat (penny ice and cold meat) to a party of
        friends and relations –
They're a ravenous horde – and they all came on board at Sloane
        Square and South Kensington stations.

W.S. GILBERT, *Iolanthe*, 1882

Victoria
Change for Victoria line

. . . and it seemed to Jim you weren't necessarily any happier
whichever side of Victoria Station you were born on. What a lot of
miserable objects he carried luggage for – sleek, soft-voiced young men
trailing behind old aunts bored to death because they were travelling
abroad. Why, the very labels excited him: Paris, Milan, Rome, Geneva,
Vienna, Bucharest, Athens, Cairo, Baghdad. If his bag ever had one of
those labels on it he'd run all the way down the platform instead of
drawling – 'Aw portah!' or 'How frightfully crowded!' or 'Really, my
dear, it's preposterous!'

Lots of things were preposterous, but not having your luggage carried down the platform, with a Venice label on it, and a first-class seat
to lounge in, and a first-class restaurant to eat in, and nothing to do
but sit and glide away out of smoke into sunshine.

CECIL ROBERTS, *Victoria Four-Thirty*, 1937

St. James's Park

Julian felt his heart beat uncommonly thick, as if conscious of
approaching someone of the highest consequence [King Charles II].

The person whom he looked upon was past the middle age of life, of a dark complexion, corresponding with the long, black, full-bottomed periwig, which he wore instead of his own hair. His dress was plain black velvet, with a diamond star, however, on his cloak, which hung carelessly over one shoulder. His features, strongly lined, even to harshness, had yet an expresssion of dignified good-humour; he was well and strongly built, walked upright and yet easily, and had upon the whole the air of a person of the highest consideration. He kept rather in advance of his companions, but turned and spoke to them, from time to time, with much affability, and probably with some liveliness, judging by the smiles, and sometimes the scarce restrained laughter, by which some of his sallies were received by his attendants. . . . They shared the attention of their principal in common with seven or eight little black curl-haired spaniels . . . whose gambols, which seemed to afford him much amusement, he sometimes regulated, and sometimes encouraged. In addition to this pastime, a lacquey, or groom, was also in attendance, with one or two little baskets and bags, from which the gentleman we have described took, from time to time, a handful of seeds, and amused himself with throwing them to the water-fowl.

SIR WALTER SCOTT, *Peveril of the Peak*, 1822,
describing Charles II in St James's Park

Westminster

Mortality, behold and feare
What a change of flesh is here!
Thinke how many royall bones
Sleep within these heap of stones;
Here they lie, had realmes and lands,
Who now want strength to stir their hands;
Where from their pulpits seal'd with dust
They preach, 'In greatness is no trust.'
Here's an acre sown indeed,
With the richest, royallst seed,
That the earth did e'er suck in,
Since the first man dy'd for sin.

FRANCIS BEAUMONT, 'On the Tombes in Westminster',
printed anonymously in 1619

He, like to a high strecht lute string squeakt, 'O Sir,
Tis sweet to talke of Kings.' 'At Westminster,'
Said I, 'The man that keepes the Abbey tombes,
And for his price doth with who ever comes,
Of all our Harries, and our Edwards talke,
From King to King and all their kin can walke:
Your eares shall heare nought, but Kings; your eyes meet
Kings only.'

JOHN DONNE, 'Satyre IIII', 1633

London is literally new to me; new in its streets, houses, and even in its situation; as the Irishman said, 'London is now gone out of town.' What I left open fields, producing hay and corn, I now find covered with streets, and squares, and palaces, and churches. I am credibly informed, that in the space of seven years, eleven thousand new houses have been built in one quarter of Westminster, exclusive of what is daily added to other parts of this unwieldy metropolis. Pimlico and Knightsbridge are now almost joined to Chelsea and Kensington; and if this infatuation continues for half a century, I suppose the whole county of Middlesex will be covered with brick.

TOBIAS SMOLLETT, *The Expedition of Humphry Clinker*, 1771

Embankment
Change for Bakerloo and Northern lines

The Great Frost was, historians tell us, the most severe that has ever visited these islands. Birds froze in mid-air and fell like stones to the ground. . . .

But while the country people suffered the extremity of want, and the trade of the country was at a standstill, London enjoyed a carnival of the utmost brilliancy. The Court was at Greenwich, and the new King seized the opportunity that his coronation gave him to curry favour with the citizens. He directed that the river, which was frozen to a depth of twenty feet and more for six or seven miles on either side, should be swept, decorated and given all the semblance of a park or pleasure ground, with arbours, mazes, alleys, drinking booths, etc., at his expense. . . . Coloured balloons hovered motionless in the air. Here and there burnt vast bonfires of cedar and oak wood, lavishly salted, so that the flames were of green, orange, and purple fire. But however fiercely they burnt, the heat was not enough to melt the ice which, though of singular transparency, was yet of the hardness of steel. So clear indeed was it that there could be seen, congealed at a depth of several feet, here a porpoise, there a flounder. Shoals of eels lay motionless in a trance, but whether their state was one of death or merely of suspended animation which the warmth would revive puzzled the philosophers. Near London Bridge, where the river had frozen to a depth of some twenty fathoms, a wrecked wherry boat was plainly visible, lying on the bed of the river where it had sunk last autumn, overladen with apples. The old bumboat woman, who was carrying her fruit to market on the Surrey side, sat there in her plaids and far-thingales with her lap full of apples, for all the world as if she were about to serve a customer, though a certain blueness about the lips hinted the truth. . . . But it was at night that the carnival was at its merriest. For the frost continued unbroken; the nights were of perfect stillness; the moon and stars blazed with the hard fixity of diamonds, and to the fine music of flute and trumpet the courtiers danced.

VIRGINIA WOOLF, *Orlando*, 1928

Temple

There are, still, worse places than the Temple, on a sultry day, for basking in the sun, or resting idly in the shade. There is yet a drowsiness in its courts, and a dreamy dullness in its streets and gardens; those who pace its lanes and squares may yet hear the echoes of their footsteps on the sounding stones, and read upon its gates, in passing from the tumult of the Strand or Fleet Street, 'Who enters here leaves noise behind.' There is still the plash of falling water in fair Fountain Court. . . . There is yet, in the Temple, something of a clerkly monkish atmosphere.

CHARLES DICKENS, *Barnaby Rudge*, 1841

Gray's Inn for Walks,
Lincoln's Inn for a Wall,
Inner Temple for a Garden,
And the Middle for a Hall.

Old rhyme quoted by James Bone in *The London Perambulator*, 1925

Blackfriars

Seven Black Friars sitting back to back
Fished from the bridge for a pike or a jack.
The first caught a tiddler, the second caught a crab,
The third caught a winkle, the fourth caught a dab,
The fifth caught a tadpole, the sixth caught an eel,
And the seventh one caught an old cart-wheel.

ELEANOR FARJEON, *Nursery Rhymes of London Town*, 1916

Mansion House

The Lord Mayor, in the stronghold of the mighty Mansion House, gave orders to his fifty cooks and butlers to keep Christmas as a Lord Mayor's household should.

CHARLES DICKENS, *A Christmas Carol*, 1843

Cannon Street

Every morning, trains disgorge thousands of city workers at Cannon Street station, a few yards east of the hidden mouth of the Walbrook, where the men of Rouen landed their cargoes a thousand years ago.

The passengers step out into a street known by the 1180s as Candlewick Street, the home of the candle-wick makers. Many go straight along Walbrook, keeping some fifty yards east of the stream, which flows more than thirty feet underground; the name itself means 'stream of the Britons' and is London's sole reminder of the old population, whom the English called Weales and who are now commemorated in Wales.

TIMOTHY BAKER, Mediaeval London, 1970

Monument

Change for escalator to Bank station for Central and Northern lines

. . . two people came to see the Monument. They were a gentleman and a lady; and the gentleman said, 'How much a-piece?'

The Man in the Monument replied, 'A Tanner.'

It seemed a low expression, compared with the Monument.

The gentleman put a shilling into his hand, and the Man in the Monument opened the dark little door. When the gentleman and lady had passed out of view, he shut it again, and came slowly back to his chair.

He sat down and laughed.

'They don't know what a many steps there is!' he said, 'It's worth twice the money to stop here. Oh, my eye!'

CHARLES DICKENS, Martin Chuzzlewit, 1843–4

Tower Hill

Change for Circle line

Baroness Orczy conceived the idea of *The Scarlet Pimpernel* in the booking hall of Tower Hill station.

. . . we all went to the next house upon Tower hill, to see the coming by of the Russia Embassador – for whose reception all the City trained bands do attend in the streets, and the King's Lifeguards, and most of the wealthy citizens in their black velvet coats and gold chains. . . . I could not see the Embassador in his coach – but his attendants in their habbits and fur caps very handsome comely men, and most of them with Hawkes upon their fists to present to the King. But Lord, to see the absurd nature of Englishmen, that cannot forbear laughing and jeering at everything that looks strange.

SAMUEL PEPYS, *Diary, 27 November 1662*

Aldgate East
Change for Hammersmith & City line

Gates in the wall of this City of old Time were Four; to wit, Aldgate for the East; Aldersgate for the North; Ludgate for the West; and the Bridge-gate, over the River of Thames for the South.

JOHN STOW, *Survey of London and Westminster*, 1598

Whitechapel
Change for East London line

Two Sticks and Apple
Ring ye Bells at Whitechapple

Tommy Thumb's Pretty Song Book, 1774

I spent a most interesting afternoon with Mary in Whitechapel. Lizzie and I went by underground and walked along Whitechapel Road to Mayfield House. How curious those streets are! There were booths all along the edge of the pavement, it looked like a great fair right down the road. The people were fascinating to watch. I should have liked to walk up and down the street for hours. . . . I think I shall buy all my clothes in Whitechapel – I saw some splendid hats loaded with ostrich feathers for 5/11; and cloaks at the same price! March 6, 1891.

GERTRUDE BELL, *The Earlier Letters of Gertrude Bell*
collected and edited by Elsa Richmond, 1937

Stepney Green

I think Stepney is a very smokey place
But I like it
People in Stepney do things wrong

But I like them
Everything in Stepney has its disadvantages
But I like it.
It does not have clean air like the country
But I like it
The buildings are old and cold
But I like them
The summer is not very hot
But I like it.

ROSEMARIE DALE, 'Stepney', *Stepney Words I and II*, 1973

Mile End
Change for Central line

By this time they had reached the turnpike at Mile End; a profound silence prevailed, until they had got two or three miles further on, when Mr. Weller senior turning suddenly to Mr. Pickwick, said –

'Wery queer life is a pike-keeper's, Sir.'

'A what?' said Mr. Pickwick.

'A pike-keeper.'

'What do you mean by a pike-keeper?' enquired Mr. Peter Magnus.

'The old 'un means a turnpike keeper, gen'l'm'n,' observed Mr. Weller, in explanation.

'Oh,' said Mr. Pickwick, 'I see. Yes; very curious life. Very uncomfortable.'

'They're all on 'em, men as has met vith some disappointment in life,' said Mr. Weller senior.

'Ay, ay?' said Mr. Pickwick.

'Yes. Consequence of vich, they retires from the world, and shuts themselves up in pikes; partly vith the view of being solitary, and partly to rewenge themselves on mankind, by takin' tolls.'

'Dear me,' said Mr. Pickwick, 'I never knew that before.'

'Fact, Sir,' said Mr. Weller; 'if they was gen'l'm'n you'd call 'em misanthropes, but as it is they only takes to pike-keepin'.'

With such conversation, possessing the inestimable charm of blending amusement with instruction, did Mr. Weller beguile the tediousness of the journey, during the greater part of the day.

CHARLES DICKENS, *The Pickwick Papers*, 1836–7

Bow Road

There was an Old Person of Bow,
Whom nobody happened to know;
So they gave him some Soap,
And said coldly, 'We hope
You will go back directly to Bow!'

EDWARD LEAR, *More Nonsense, Pictures, Rhymes, Botany, etc.*, 1872

You owe me five farthings,
Say the bells of St Martin's.

When will you pay me?
Say the bells of Old Bailey.

I'm sure I don't know,
Says the great bell at Bow.

Tommy Thumb's Pretty Song Book, 1774

Bromley-by-Bow

Adjoining Bow in the south-east, in the parish of Bromley . . . a short distance northwards of the church, a large brick-built mansion – one of the former glories of the place – is still standing. . . . It is commonly known as the Old Palace* . . .

Before quitting Bromley we must not omit to mention the bowling-green, the village stocks, the whipping-post, the pond and ducking-stool, and the parish pound, all of which remained in full operation down to the latter part of the last century.

E. WALFORD, *Greater London*, 1882–4

* remembered in the lines:

Outside there's nothing now to show
The house was built so long ago:
But inside you will see,
The pendant ceiling, pannel'd wall,
Rich chimnies, Royal arms and all
Just as it used to be.
Then all was country around,
The forest near – then open ground
With Stebonheath close by.
And hunting was the favourite sport,
Of James the first, and all his court:
To make the hours fly.

West Ham

The story of West Ham's Football Club begins over fifty years ago. Not with the founding of a professional club but with the formation of a works team. Which is as it should be, for ever since these earliest days the West Ham club has found its supporters among the people of London's busiest, most hard-worked area. The Club belongs to the crowded streets, the docksides, the manufactures, the print shops and transport depots of East London. West Ham United is truly of the place and the people. . . . A crowd that urges on the home side with shouts of 'Come on, the Hammers!' and cries of 'Up the Irons!' will clearly have no time for showy stuff on the field. The club has always got most of its players 'over the wall' from the back streets of East London and from the playing fields of Essex.

REG GROVES, *Official History of West Ham United*, 1947

Plaistow

Upon a fertile Spot of Land,
Does *Plaistow*, thriving *Plaistow*, stand:
The Sea, which whilom roll'd his Flood,
And hither brought the fat'ning Mud,
Has left a Richness in the Soil
That well rewards the Peasant's Toil.
One side the Level Marshes sees,
And all is interspers'd with Trees:
From hence the Silver *Thames* appears,
And the wing'd Vessels which she bears; . . .
A pleasing Sight, to see them ride
With Sails unfurl'd, with Wind and Tide.
From hence to our delighted Eyes,
Does Greenwich' Royal Spires arise; . . .

With wholsome Fare our Villa's stor'd;
Our Lands the best of Corn afford;
Nor Hertford Wheat, nor Derby Rye,
Nor Ipswich Pease, can our's outvye:
The largest Ox that *England* bred,
Was in our verdant Pastures fed.

Let *Irish* Wights no longer boast
The fam'd Potatoes of their Coast:
Potatoes now are *Plaistow's* Pride;
Whole Markets are from hence supply'd,
Nor finer Mutton can you spend,
Than what our fat'ning Marshes send,
And in our Farmers Yards you find,
Delicious Fowls of divers Kind;
Whose Cellars rarely ever fail,
To keep a Cask of Nappy Ale.

In Praise of Plaistow in the County of Essex. A Poem, 1753

Upton Park

Upton, Wimbledon, Elm and St. James
All share 'Park' in their station names.
Parsons and Stepney and Turnham 'Green'
Add fields and lawns to the rural scene.
And you feel the magic of Richmond and Kew?
Then the Green District Line is the line for you.

ANON.

East Ham

The [Tudor] mansion's popular name Boleyn Castle came from the erroneous tradition that Anne Boleyn lived here during Henry's courtship. . . . The immediate area is colloquially known as 'The Boleyn' and modern roads to the east are named after Henry VIII's wives and Anne's brother Lord Rochford.

The London Encyclopaedia edited by Ben Weinreb
and Christopher Hibbert, 1983

Barking

We saw passing from Barking to Dagenham, the famous Breach, made by an Inundation of the Thames, which was so great, that it laid near

5000 Acres of Land under Water, but which after near ten Years lying in that manner, and being several times blown up, has been at last effectually stopped by the application of Captain Perry; the Gentleman, who for several Years had been employed, in the Czar of Muscovy's Works, at Veronitza, on the river Don. This Breach appeared now effectually made up, and they assured us, that the new Work, where the Breach was, is by much esteemed the strongest of all the Sea Walls in that Level.

DANIEL DEFOE, *A Tour thro' the Whole Island of Great Britain*, 1738

Upney

Just 'Upney', reads the station sign,
Out eastward, on the District Line,
Which, one stop short of Becontree,
Is thirty-two from Gunnersbury.

Now who was Upney, one might ask;
Was once a death-defying task
Performed, by which this humble name
In ticket booths achieved such fame?

Avoid the next stop, Becontree,
For beckoning trees mean devilry,
Such trees can only signal death,
As those which stalked the cruel Macbeth.

Best stick to Upney, keep it short,
Do not befriend the Barking sort,
For dogs or persons barking mad
Could well attack the shin or head.

Dear modest Upney, so petite,
As comfy as a railway seat;
An Upney simple, Upney slow,
Non-uppity as your Auntie Flo.

So why continue to Elm Park,
Why head for Dagenham's booking clerk
Where Upney begs a passing stop,
As might, of poets, Adlestrop.

Just 'Auntie', reads the station sign –
For Upney, on the District Line,
An Upney which, so upney small,
Seems upney to exist at all.

MONICA HOYER, 'Upney, the Name', 1994

Becontree

Becontree is named after the beacon that was lit at the approach of the Armada.

Night sank upon the dusky beach, and on the purple sea,
Such night in England ne'er had been, nor e'er again shall be.
From Eddystone to Berwick bounds, from Lynn to Milford Bay,
That time of slumber was as bright and busy as the day;
For swift to east and swift to west the ghastly war-flame spread,
High on St. Michael's Mount it shone: it shone on Beachy Head.
Far on the deep the Spaniard saw, along each southern shire,
Cape beyond cape, in endless range, those twinkling points of fire . . .
From all the batteries of the Tower peeled loud the voice of fear;
And all the thousand masts of Thames sent back a louder cheer . . .
And on and on, without a pause, untired they bounded still:
All night from tower to tower they sprang; they sprang from hill to hill.

THOMAS BABINGTON, LORD MACAULAY,
from 'The Armada', *Lays of Ancient Rome*, 1842

Dagenham Heathway

A little beyond the Town, on the Road to Dagenham, stood a great House, antient, and now almost fallen down, where Tradition says, the *Gunpowder-Treason Plot* was at first contriv'd, and that all the first Consultations about it were held there.

DANIEL DEFOE, *A Tour thro' the Whole Island of Great Britain*, 1724–6

Dagenham East

On the way to the coast for cockles they pass the Ford plant at Dagenham, that Detroit moonscape where every man's car is processed out; they inch past it choking each other to death with their fumes. The dream of the bright young things, fast and furious whirling through the countryside, twists round all our throats like Isadora Duncan's scarf. The lady and the motoring veil: there's a dance macabre for a brave choreographer.

MAUREEN DUFFY, *Capital*, 1975

Elm Park

Elm Park . . . takes its name from natural local woodland.

CYRIL M. HARRIS, What's in a Name?, 1977

Hornchurch

On Christmas-day, the following custom has been observed at Hornchurch, in Essex, from time immemorial. The lessee of the tithes, which belong to New College, Oxford, supplies a boar's head dressed, and garnished with bay-leaves etc. In the afternoon, it is carried in procession into the Mill Field, adjoining the church-yard, where it is wrestled for; and it is afterwards feasted upon, at one of the public-houses, by the rustic conqueror and his friends, with all the merriment peculiar to the season.

WILLIAM HONE, The Every-Day Book and Table Book, 1830,
entry for 25 December

Upminster Bridge

. . . there is a small iron road bridge, marked Upminster Bridge. Tradition has it that the Romans built a ford here over the River Ingrebourne during Caesar's invasion of England. It seeems that in *c.*1300 a wooden bridge was built to replace the ford.

CYRIL M. HARRIS, What's in a Name?, 1977

Upminster

Upminster Tithe Barn Hall Lane . . . dates from about the middle of the 15th century. It stands near the drive to Upminster Hall and was probably used by the monks of Waltham Abbey. . . . It has been made into a museum of agricultural and local history.

The London Encyclopaedia edited by Ben Weinreb
and Christopher Hibbert, 1983

ACKNOWLEDGEMENTS

We would like to thank our families and friends who have helped us over the years during the prepaation of this book, especially Sandy Marriage, Robin Ollington, Bryan Rooney, Suzanne St Albans, Anthony Sampson, Kathleen Tillotson, Malcolm Holmes of the Camden Local History Library and the staff of the North Reading Room, British Library.

The compilers and publishers gratefully acknowledge permission to reproduce the following copyright material in this book:

Fleur Adcock: 'Miss Hamilton in London' from *Selected Poems* (1983), © Oxford University Press 1967. Originally published in *Tigers*, 1967. Reprinted by permission of Oxford University Press.

Timothy Baker: *Mediaeval London*, © Timothy Baker 1970. Reprinted by permission of Cassell.

Max Beerbohm: *And Even Now*, © Max Beerbohm 1920. Reprinted by permission of Mrs Reichmann.

J.A. Brooks: *Ghosts of London*, © J.A. Brooks 1982. Reprinted by permission of Jarrold Publishing.

John Carey: *Original Copy*, © John Carey 1987. Reprinted by permission of Faber & Faber.

Rosemarie Dale: 'Stepney' from *Stepney Words I and II*, © Rosemarie Dale 1973. Reprinted by permission of Centreprise Publications.

Maureen Duffy: *Capital*, © Maureen Duffy 1975. Reprinted by permission of Jonathan Cape.

Gavin Ewart: 'Earl's Court' from *Londoners*, © Gavin Ewart 1964. Reprinted by permission of William Heinemann.

Alethea Hayter: *A Sultry Month: Scenes of London Literary Life in 1846*. © Alethea Hayter 1965. Reprinted by permission of Robin Clark.

John Heath-Stubbs: *Satires and Epigrams*, © John Heath-Stubbs 1968. Reprinted by permission of David Higham Associates.

Philip Howard: 'Wapping' and 'Philip Howard looks at London' from *The Times*, © Times Newspapers. Reprinted by permission of Times Newspapers.

Monica Hoyer: 'Upney, the Name', © Monica Hoyer 1994.

John Mortimer: 'Rumpole and the Sprit of Christmas' from *Rumpole for the Defence*, © Ad van Press Ltd 1981. Reprinted by permission of Penguin Books.

Cecil Roberts: *Victoria Four-Thirty*, © Cecil Roberts 1937. Reprinted by permission of Hodder & Stoughton.

C.H. Rolph: *London Particulars*, © C.H. Rolph 1980. Published by Oxford University Press. Reprinted by permission of David Higham Associates.

Richard Trench and Ellis Hillman: *London Under London*, © Richard Trench and Ellis Hillman 1984, 1993. Reprinted by permission of John Murray.

Ben Weinreb and Christopher Hibbert: *The London Encyclopaedia*, © Ben Weinreb and Christopher Hibbert 1983. Reprinted by permission of Macmillan London.

H.G. Wells: *Tono-Bungay*. © H.G. Wells 1909. Reprinted by permission of A.P. Watt on behalf of The Literary Executors of the Estate of H.G. Wells.

The publishers have made every effort to contact copyright holders where they can be found. The publishers will be happy to include any missing copyright acknowledgements in future editions.
